CONTENTS

Some words are shown in bold, **like this**. You can find out what they mean by looking in the glossary.

BE AN INVENTOR!

Take a look around you. Many of the things that you can see were invented. From the wheels on your bicycle to the television in your house, an inventor dreamed them up and brought their ideas to life. Inventors are **curious** and imaginative people. If you dream of inventing new machines and **gadgets**, then dream big!

Inspiration

Get yourself a notebook and start your own 'Inventor's Secret **Journal**'. Write down all of your brilliant ideas!

Dream It, Do It!

GET INVENTING!

Mary Colson

raintree

Raintree is an imprint of Capstone Global Library Limited, a company incorporated in England and Wales having its registered office at 7 Pilgrim Street, London, EC4V 6LB – Registered company number: 6695582

www.raintreepublishers.co.uk
myorders@raintreepublishers.co.uk

Edited by Rebecca Rissman, Dan Nunn, and Helen Cox Cannons
Designed by Steve Mead
Original illustrations © Capstone Global Library
Picture research by Ruth Blair
Production by Vicki Fitzgerald
Originated by Capstone Global Library Ltd
Printed and bound in China

ISBN 978 1 406 27262 8 (hardback)
18 17 16 15 14
10 9 8 7 6 5 4 3 2 1

ISBN 978 1 406 27267 3 (paperback)
19 18 17 16 15 14
10 9 8 7 6 5 4 3 2 1

British Library Cataloguing in Publication Data
A full catalogue record for this book is available from the British Library.

Acknowledgements
We would like to thank the following for permission to reproduce photographs: Capstone Publishers pp. 21, 26–29 (all © Karon Dubke); FLPA p. 23 (Nicholas and Sherry Lu Aldridge); Getty Images pp. 5 (MJ Kim), 24 (Hulton Archive); Shutterstock pp. 6 (© Africa Studio), 7 (© Christopher Edwin Nuzzaco), 8 left (© Rob Byron), 8 right (© colorvsbw), 9 (© Edwin Verin), 11 top (© IM_photo), 11 bottom (© Zurijeta), 12 left (© Vorobyeva), 12 middle (© Cherkas), 12 bottom (© Sergiy Telesh); 13 (© fabio fersa), 14 (© Jason Vandehey), 15 (© Poznyakov), 16 (xxxxxxxx), 17 (© Kamil Macniak), 18 (© ffolas), 19 (© Ivonne Wierink), 20 (© wawritto), 22 (© djem), 25 (© Andrey_Kuzmin), 25 (© Stocksnapper).
Incidental photographs reproduced with permission of Shutterstock.
Cover photograph of a woman flying reproduced with permission of Getty Images (Westend61).

Every effort has been made to contact copyright holders of material reproduced in this book. Any omissions will be rectified in subsequent printings if notice is given to the publisher.

Disclaimer
All the Internet addresses (URLs) given in this book were valid at the time of going to press. However, due to the dynamic nature of the Internet, some addresses may have changed, or sites may have changed or ceased to exist since publication. While the author and publisher regret any inconvenience this may cause readers, no responsibility for any such changes can be accepted by either the author or the publisher.

GETTING GREAT IDEAS

Inventors are always on the lookout for new ideas. They try to improve everyday objects we already have or they create brand new things.

Cut out pictures from magazines of inventions you like. The pictures can show small things, such as kitchen **utensils**, or big things, such as cars. Stick the pictures in your **journal**. Write down what it is about the objects that works well. Think about how you could improve them.

IMPROVING WHAT'S THERE

Most inventions are improvements on existing items or ways of doing things. For example, if a tool or **utensil** doesn't work as well as it should, an inventor will think about how to improve it.

Think about the objects you use in the hobbies and activities in your life. Can you think of any ways in which the objects could be improved?

TACKLING PROBLEMS

Inventors need time, patience, and open minds to make their inventions work. They also need to respond to what people suggest or advise. For example, the aeroplane was invented after a lot of practice, changes, and experiments.

Activity

Invent a new type of flying machine and draw it in your inventor's **journal**. What shape will the machine be? What **fuel** will it use? What will it be made of?

You can't actually try out your flying machine but you can ask friends to look at your design. Can they see any problems with it?

TESTING MATERIALS

Inventors work with all kinds of materials, such as wood, plastic, steel, and brick. They think about which materials will be best for the object's purpose. After all, it's no use making a teapot out of chocolate!

Imagine you're going to invent a new type of boat. First, you will need to test out some materials. Try floating different materials in your bath to see which will be the best for your invention. **Review** your floating test. Which was the best material for your boat? Why?

INVENTOR'S STUDIO

Most inventors have a studio or space where they do their most top-secret work. Some inventors work in **laboratories** and some even work under ground.

Create a space where you can sit, think, and write down ideas. You will need pens, paper, and your inventor's **journal**. Make sure your space is safe from pets and younger brothers or sisters!

HELPING OTHERS

Inventors work to make life easier for everybody. Imagine having a machine that tidied your bedroom in 5 minutes!

Activity

Ask people in your family about what they would find useful. A new type of stirrer for cooking with? A **gadget** to pick up slippery spaghetti? A duster that reaches the top shelf? Think about what the object would be used for and how you would make it work.

COOKING UP A TREAT!

Did you know you can invent new recipes? Chefs are always thinking creatively to invent new and tasty dishes.

Activity

In your inventor's **journal**, draw some cupcakes with some new toppings. Remember to label your cake with the **ingredients** and flavours you would use. Why not try some unusual flavours and colours?

With an adult's help, make some cupcakes and test out your ideas using different ingredients for toppings. You might be surprised by what works! Get your family to taste test your cakes.

ECO-INVENTIONS

Modern inventors often try to recycle objects and make them into new, usable items. Can you think of something new to make from an object that you would usually throw away?

Activity

In your inventor's studio, take a plastic food tray, some paper, sticky tape or glue, and pens. Make this into a new object, such as a desk tidy. Think about what the finished object has to do.

Did your invention work? Could it be improved? Note down your findings in your inventor's **journal**.

WATER-WISE INVENTIONS

A key issue for the inventors of today and tomorrow is using **natural resources**, such as water, wisely.

Water metre

Activity

Invent an object that collects rainwater, which can be used to water indoor plants with. You could use plastic from your recycling box at home.

What worked and what didn't work? Did you get enough water for your plants? Make notes in your inventor's **journal** and think about how you could improve your invention.

Rain catcher

PRACTICE MAKES PERFECT!

Not all inventions work straight away, or even at all. Even inventors need to practise inventing! Famous inventors such as Thomas Edison, who invented the light bulb, created lots of things that worked but many more that didn't.

One of the first ever aeroplanes, invented by the Wright brothers.

Activity

Look back through your inventor's **journal**. Which of your inventions was most successful? Is there a particular invention you want to develop? Which one do you think could make the most difference to people's lives?

Try making that idea out of different materials. Can you improve on what you've already done?

GAME MASTER!

Every year, inventors carefully plan and create exciting new toys and games for people to enjoy. Imagine that a toy company has asked you to invent a new board game for a family to play. Follow these simple steps to help you get started:

1. In your inventor's **journal**, write down what the purpose of the game is. Is it to win money or property? Is it to be first round the board?

2. How many players will your game be for?

3. How do players move around the board? Do they throw dice?

4. Think about the board's design. What does it look like?

5. What will stop a player from winning? What are the traps?

6. Do you need to write **forfeit cards**?

7. Do you need to design game money or tokens?

8. How will you know who the winner is?

Explain the rules of your game to a friend. Play the game together. Did they suggest any improvements? Does the board design work?

GLOSSARY

curious keen to know things

forfeit card card that forces someone to give up something in a board game

fuel energy or power, such as petrol

gadget small tool with a clever design

ingredients food items in a recipe

journal written record of a person's thoughts and experiences

laboratory place used for scientific testing

natural resources materials that are found in nature, such as coal, wood, and water

review look back at something that has already taken place and see what went wrong or right

utensil cooking tool

FIND OUT MORE

Books

Incredible Inventions, Lee Bennett Hopkins (Greenwillow Books, 2009)

Tony Robinson's Weird World of Wonders: Inventions, Tony Robinson (Macmillan, 2013)

Websites

www.coolkidscooking.com

Start inventing in your kitchen! Visit this site for recipes and cooking ideas to get you started.

www.inventivekids.com

Read about inventions, play invention games, and get inspired!

INDEX